Crossing Borders:
A Job Seeker's Guide to Humanitarian Work

Silper Pesa

Crossing Borders: A Job Seeker's Guide to Humanitarian Work
© 2024 by Silper Pesa
SilperPesa@Ascenda.Store
Crossing Borders: A Job Seeker's Guide to Humanitarian Work / Silper Pesa

For permission requests, write to the publisher, addressed "Attention: Permissions Coordinator," at the address below:
Maasaiaivisions LLC
1209 Mountain Road PL NE, #4615
Albuquerque, New Mexico, 87110
maasaiaivisions@gmail.com
Business: SilperPesa@Ascenda.Store
Library of Congress Cataloging-in-Publication Data
Library of Congress Control Number: 2024947889

Crossing Borders: A Job Seeker's Guide to Humanitarian Work
Silper Pesa
Published by wclarkpublishing.com
Hardcover: 978-1-957954-69-1
eBook: 978-1-957954-70-7
Audiobook: 978-1-957954-71-4

Cover design by www.nuanceartllc.com.
Edited by Nerissa Otumba

Printed in the United States of America.
First Edition, October 2024

Disclaimer

The views expressed in the guidebook are those of the author and do not necessarily reflect the view of any organization.

Table of Contents

Foreword

In "Crossing Borders: A Job Seeker's guide to Humanitarian Work," Silper opens the door to her world, a world filled with resilience, empathy, and an unyielding commitment to serving others. Her journey is a remarkable blend of courage, determination, and an unshakeable belief in the power of compassion. I first met Silper in Yangon, Myanmar, far from our shared roots in Kenya. We were both drawn to this path by a mutual desire to make a difference. What began as a chance encounter blossomed into a friendship marked by shared values and a deep understanding of the challenges and triumphs that come with working in humanitarian contexts. Over the years, I've seen Silper's dedication grow stronger, her spirit unwavering, and her ability to impact the lives of those around her truly inspirational.

Reading this book has been a humbling experience for me. Silper's voice shines through every page, sharing her journey with authenticity, humor, and an inspiring sense of purpose. She doesn't shy away from the hard truths but instead uses them to guide, uplift, and encourage those who dream of making a similar impact. For anyone considering a path in humanitarian work, this book serves as a beacon, illuminating the road ahead with practical wisdom, heartfelt stories, and a clear message: it's possible to make a difference, no matter how daunting the journey may seem. Silper's journey is a testament to what one person can achieve with passion, determination, and an unwavering love for humanity. I am honored to share this journey with her and to introduce you to her incredible story. –

Rosemary Owino, Senior Financial Management Expert with 25+years' experience in the NGO sector, currently, FM Specialist at Gavi, the vaccine alliance.

Acknowledgments

My greatest appreciation goes to Karen Chuk, the AI consultant, who sat next to me at the John Maxwell certification in Orlando on that fine morning in March 2024. It was nothing short of the divine intervention, I hold close to my heart. Next, I was introduced to the AI certification Training run by Alicia Lyttle and her sister Lorette, who opened the doors through the 3-day AI Summit held in April 2024, where I met Wahida Clark and Anitra Lane through subsequent discovery calls. Special Thanks to Rosemary Owino, my mentor and someone I looked up-to in my career for the prelude. All these people have guided me through the intricate steps of leveraging AI and eventually publishing this book. Knowing you all has taught me the importance of networking. Your support and encouragement have been invaluable, and I am deeply grateful to each of you.

Thank you to all the dedicated readers interested in my book, crafted for aspiring and seasoned humanitarian workers, students, professionals transitioning into the sector, and those seeking meaningful post-retirement roles. Drawing from my experiences in 13 countries across six organizations, this book offers practical guidance, career strategies, and insights into the complexities of joining and thriving in humanitarian work. I hope it empowers you, deepens your understanding, and equips you to advance your career and make a lasting impact.

My deepest gratitude goes to my two daughters, Melissa and Golden, and my family. You have loved me as I am, with all my faults, and never judged my decisions, no matter how questionable or crazy they may have seemed. Thank you for being my unwavering support system. And thank you, J.J. for always being my cheerleader.

- Silper Pesa

THE GUIDEBOOK

Embark on a transformative journey from volunteer to humanitarian worker with "Crossing Borders: A Job Seekers Guide to Humanitarian Work". Drawing from over twenty years of firsthand experience and spanning thirteen countries, this guidebook offers practical insight, valuable lessons, and actionable advice for aspiring humanitarian professionals.

I use the term 'humanitarian worker' to refer to employment across humanitarian, development or peace-building networks, including in emergencies elicited by natural disasters, conflicts, or other crises. These individuals provide essential services, including medical care, food, water, shelter, and education. Typically, these humanitarian workers work for NGOs, international aid agencies, or multinational organizations like the United Nations and may operate domestically and internationally. The humanitarian worker role demands resilience and adaptability, as conditions can be challenging and potentially hazardous.

Whether you are a recent graduate, career changer, or seasoned professional seeking to transition into humanitarian work, this book will equip you with the knowledge and tools needed to navigate the complex world of an international humanitarian worker and make a meaningful impact.

Navigating any career can be challenging and filled with unexpected hurdles and setbacks. I have faced numerous falls, but what defines my journey is my resilience to rise each time.

My humanitarian work was not a walk in the park, and yours won't be either. Success requires knowing the direction you want to take and consistently putting in the effort. John Maxwell's Law of Intentionality reminds us that growth does not just happen; it requires intention and deliberate action. So, embrace the trials, persist through the setbacks, and stay focused on your goals, for growth is a journey that demands perseverance and purpose.

I began as a student intern and then moved on to three American NGOs: The International Rescue Committee, International Medical Corps, and Mercy Corps. After sending over fifty applications, I landed my first job with OCHA in Myanmar on a three-month contract several miles from home.

Who does that? I moved from a guaranteed role and contract to a three-month contract in a new organization away from home.

This move into an unknown territory illustrates John Maxwell's Law of the Rubber Band, which asserts that growth happens outside your comfort zone. I began my career as an intern while still an undergraduate student. After serving in four Organizations as an expatriate, I transitioned to UN Women before returning to where it all began. This move represents a full-circle moment for me, as I plan to conclude my career in the same organization where I initially found my passion as a University Student intern. This passion was sparked during a food airdrop mission to displaced persons in South Sudan. Later, I had to travel well over 6,500 Kilometers from Kenya to Myanmar to take up my first job at the United Nations.

My journey highlights the significance of perseverance and determination in overcoming numerous rejections and setbacks to achieve one's career goals.

From my experience, I wish to invite you to embark on your journey to joining and thriving in the United Nations with confidence, determination, and purpose, using "Crossing Borders: A Job Seekers Guide to Humanitarian Work" as your guide. You will be empowered to navigate the complexities of international diplomacy, make a meaningful impact as an NGO worker, and become a catalyst for positive change in the world.

SILPER PESA

Introduction

During my final year as an undergraduate student at Moi University, an ordinary encounter led to a transformative journey. I met my roommate's husband, Martin M., who worked at the Kakuma refugee camp in northern Kenya. Hearing about his experiences invoked my curiosity, stirring a desire to follow a similar path.

I contacted the head of the sub-office in Kakuma. To cut the long story short, after exchanging emails, I secured a placement in the Kakuma Refugee Camp. The prospect of working in such a dynamic environment excited me, and my ambition to mirror Martin's experiences became a driving force.

This desire resonates with John Maxwell's "Law of the Mirror", which stresses the importance of seeing value in oneself to achieve success. By believing in my potential to navigate and contribute to a challenging environment like Kakuma, I took steps that mirrored Martin's journey, demonstrating the impact of self-confidence on personal growth and achievement.

The Journey Begins

Embarking on the journey from Nairobi to Kakuma was an adventure in itself. Multiple bus rides and over forty-eight hours of waiting tested my Patience across Kitale, Kapenguria and Turkana, but the anticipation kept me going. Upon arrival in Kakuma, my Volunteer Admin/Finance Assistant role presented diverse challenges.

I supported the processing of vendor payments and handled travel allowances for South Sudanese child soldiers. This group of minors, often recruited forcibly by government forces and rebel groups, were compelled to participate in acts of violence, violating international laws and conventions. Those fortunate enough to be rescued embarked on their journey to resettlement abroad in countries like Australia, Canada, Sweden, or the United States.

Discovering Resilience in Adversity

Despite its harsh semi-arid environment, the camp provided essential infrastructure such as shelters, schools, and health Centers. Here, I witnessed firsthand the resilience and resourcefulness of South Sudanese refugees, who were primarily engaged in activities like farming, entrepreneurship, and education to sustain themselves.

While challenges like overcrowding and limited resources persisted, the camp served as a testament to the strength and determination of displaced populations striving for a better future.

A Humanitarian Mission of Impact

An opportunity presented itself and allowed me to participate in a project that targeted an international group of university students drawn from donor countries like Japan, the Netherlands, and Sweden to participate in a food airdrop in South Sudan.

The event left an indelible mark on me. Embarking on a daring humanitarian mission, our cargo plane descended through the turbulent skies over war-torn South Sudan. Loaded with life-saving goods destined for the displaced, anticipation hung heavy in the air among us, the crew, and volunteers onboard.

Witnessing the Power of Compassion

With practiced precision, heavy pallets of maize were released into the wide-open dry fields below, descending like benevolent angels amidst the chaos of conflict.

How it all began – search engine images of air food drop in Sudan

From our aerial vantage point, we could only imagine the scene unfolding on the ground and the distant sea of desperate faces awaiting the arrival of this life-sustaining cargo. Amidst the chaotic dust, the resilience of the human spirit was laid bare as individuals grasped at the chance to secure their next meal amidst the unforgiving backdrop of adversity.

Finding My Life's Purpose at Nineteen

A profound sense of purpose washed over me as we looked down upon this scene of desperation and hope. Witnessing the plight of internally displaced persons ignited a renewed resolve to contribute to humanitarian causes. From that day forward, I knew without a shadow of a doubt that this was my purpose, my reason for being—to dedicate my life to serving others, to lending a helping hand to those displaced and marginalized by the cruelties of conflict and hardship.

Each day, I reaffirm my commitment to humanitarian work as I witness the resilience of communities facing unimaginable challenges. It's a constant reminder that even in the darkest times, there is hope, and every small act of kindness can have a ripple effect that extends far beyond what we can imagine.

Trials at Home

Reflecting on my experience, I am grateful for the opportunity to have taken the trip alongside like-minded incredible teenagers and been a part of something significant. Back at the university, I channelled these new experiences and the desperate need to make a difference into advocacy through the newly founded Refugee Welfare Club. As a minor subject at the university, I delved deep into Refugee Law studies, seeking to broaden my understanding of the principles guiding our humanitarian efforts. I was introduced to among other guidelines, the principle of 'non-refoulement' that prohibits sending refugees back to a country where they face threats of persecution or harm.

Embracing the Journey

As fate would have it, after graduation, I competed and was offered a role as an accountant with the International Rescue Committee (IRC). In my journey, I observed the quick rise of a young American lady named Nicole W. from a Program Officer to a Program Manager, within a year of service. She challenged me and I knew this was something worth emulating. The question was not if this was possible but rather 'when' remained the big question.

This experience highlighted John Maxwell's Law of Awareness from his book, "The 15 Invaluable Laws of Growth," which emphasizes recognizing and understanding one's strengths, weaknesses, and passions to set goals and progress.

Maxwell's law resonates with this observation, demonstrating how personal awareness and clarity can lead to tangible career progression. I kept an eye on Nicole's career progression from a distance. My continued search for Nicole online over the years illustrates the significance of tracking one's path and monitoring others' growth, which can inspire and motivate one's journey forward.

By embodying the law of awareness, you too, can align your goals with your passions, embrace growth opportunities, and achieve new heights in your career. Years later, when I followed her progress on LinkedIn, I noticed that Nicole had become a Country Director, unknowingly inspiring my dream to pursue an expatriate career. I knew it was only a matter of time.

To paraphrase Arnold H. Glasgow's sentiment in a fresh way, you could say, "Patience is the master key to every opportunity. Just as an egg needs time and care to bring forth a chick, our endeavors require a gentle, patient hand to reach successful outcomes rather than being rushed."

In April 2024, I searched on LinkedIn to see how far Nicole had progressed professionally and reached out to let her know how she had continued to inspire me unknowingly. She would be a part of this book that I had been putting up together. I continued with the belief that with focus, I could also achieve success, no matter how much or little it compared to Nicole. This highlighted what I learned this year about John Maxwell's Law of Modeling, which stresses the importance of learning from mentors and role models to accelerate personal growth.

I am grateful to direct and indirect mentors, such as Nicole.

These are mentors who went before me, serving humanity and inspiring others to follow in their footsteps. To those seeking to join humanitarian work or any other career path, always remember that seeking out mentors is crucial for accelerating growth and achieving success. In embracing dream makers and overcoming dream killers, I have learned the value of persistence, adaptability, and community.

Returning to Kenya from Darfur, I slowly rebuilt my life. This journey has been a testament to the resilience required to navigate the professional world and the importance of staying open to the possibilities that come from seizing every chance encounter and good deed.

My journey in the humanitarian sector has been filled with triumphs and tribulations, but my drive to make a positive impact remains unwavering. As I continue to serve this noble cause, I am reminded of Sadako's famous words: "The world is not all misery and suffering. Great people are doing great things." It is my privilege and honor to be counted among them.

A Call to Adventure

Embarking on the journey to self-improvement and personal growth is akin to stepping into a realm of boundless opportunities, where every challenge, setback, and triumph serves as a steppingstone toward becoming the best version of ourselves.

In this exhilarating adventure, you are not merely passengers, but fearless explorers, charting uncharted territories of your potential and discovering the limitless horizons of your capabilities.

Humanitarian work is a journey where the path may be uncertain, but the rewards are immeasurable. A journey that beckons us to embrace change, confront adversity, and push beyond our comfort zones in pursuit of our dreams.

Together, let us dare to dream, dare to aspire, and dare to thrive, for the possibilities are endless when we dare to be the best versions of ourselves.

The Journey of Service Across Borders

As fate would have it, after graduation, I competed and was offered a role as an accountant with the International Rescue Committee (IRC). Two years later, I took a career break to pursue my master's degree in the UK. By this time, Nicole was a Country Director. I realized that I, too, could succeed if I stayed focused.

Dream makers, like dream killers, often play significant roles in our lives, especially when it comes to career opportunities. I recall my journey with one "dream killer "- a company which I will refer to by its initials - C. A in London after my master's degree.

I had successfully competed for a role at C.A, only to have the offer rescinded two weeks later in favor of another candidate. This experience taught me the harsh reality of discrimination in the workplace, where several factors play a role beyond just one's qualifications.

Despite disclosing my nationality during the interview and the need for a work permit if offered the role, the same reasons impeded my success two weeks after the job offer. I was okay with the preference of the second candidate, who I was told was British. What I was not okay with was why I received the offer if I did not meet all the requirements, only to have the job offer rescinded two weeks later. I was crushed, but not broken. I knew I would live to see a better day. I kept the fire in my heart alive and burning.

Needless to say, the disappointment was the missing gap and the sign I needed, as it fueled my decision to pursue other competitive opportunities with international NGOs abroad, ultimately shaping my career path and keeping my dream to mirror Nicole alive.

My next experience taught me the power of seizing opportunities and building connections. During a flight to Kenya for a family funeral, a kind gesture led to a conversation with a Croatian woman named Borjana M. who introduced me to a recruitment site for international humanitarian roles.

A competitive recruitment process eventually led to a job offer from the US office of the International Medical Corps in Oregon, Portland, marking my final entry into expatriate work.

I finally made it, and you can, too, if you follow the seven steps I want to share. The encounter with a Croatian link, over thirty thousand feet above the ground, unlocked for me the 'almost impossible door till then' and reinforced the importance of formal and informal networks in the humanitarian field and how simple interactions can lead to profound opportunities. In embracing dream makers and overcoming dream killers, I have learned the value of persistence and adaptability.

Returning to Kenya from Darfur, I slowly rebuilt my life. This journey has been a testament to the resilience required to navigate the professional world and the importance of staying open to the possibilities that come from seizing every chance encounter and good deed.

A journey that began with voluntary service has seen me serve in thirteen countries to date, and I am still counting. Each destination brought its own unique challenges and opportunities, shaping my perspective and deepening my commitment to humanitarian work.

I was in Myanmar when Aung San Su Kyi was released from house arrest. I stayed on for three years and witnessed the crowds as the then-UN Secretary-General and the US President visited Myanmar.

To show how much the country opened up and the cost of living shot up, my rent, which was fifteen hundred dollars a month, tripled within three years. Initially, we went to Thailand every twenty-eight days to renew our work visa, but the country opened up gradually, and in the last year, we got a one-year visa and with that came the end of the monthly Thai fried rice –"khao pad" and shrimp soup.

I was in Darfur when President Bashir was indicted. He expelled fourteen non-profit organizations and requested all staff to vacate Sudan within forty-eight hours. Unfortunately, each agency's head of finance and program was not issued with exit visas and stayed on for a month.

The government issued a decree mandating the 14 expelled organizations to pay their national staff an additional six months' worth of salaries. This was a tough call for the expelled organizations, as these amounts were neither budgeted nor funded. The amount translated to nearly two hundred thousand dollars monthly, to be paid for six months for my organization alone.

I was at the negotiating table, later joined by the mandated chief negotiator, to support the affected NGOs. By the second week, we faced intimidation and threats from security agents. We were only released after the longest month in my entire life after the unbudgeted amounts were cleared following negotiations with donor countries.

Ironically, in 2013, when I got a job offer with UN Women, I reached the airport in Khartoum to take up my new role but was not allowed to leave. The same national intelligence had 'persona non grata' for all staff who worked for the fourteen NGOs during the expulsion. This had nothing to do with the staff per se, as none of them committed any crime, but rather, it was a thankless punishment for those who served any of the American and British NGOs expelled from Darfur, during that period. I was isolated at the airport and only released after nearly twelve hours to board the four AM flight back to Nairobi.

There was nothing we ever did. If anything, we stayed for an extra month to ensure the extra amount demanded by the government was paid. My agency later moved me to Ethiopia.

I was in Yemen when the sanctions declaration was announced. I was there during Covid-19. One colleague I supported for treatment passed away due to COVID-19, and I had to lead in repatriating his body to enable the family to give him a decent send-off.

Staying True to the Call

Staying True to the Call: Leading through Challenges

When I agreed to my humanitarian call, I knew it would not be a smooth path. However, I have stayed true to my call. In my role, I primarily lead in finding solutions to challenges faced in the operational implementation of the support given to displaced persons.

I remain faithful to my call, navigating through challenges with resilience and determination.

So far, I have served in thirteen countries, from Myanmar to Afghanistan to Yemen and even Hungary, and my journey is still ongoing. As a way of giving back, I want to share the seven steps that guided me. I hope to inspire others to follow a similar path, just as Nicole inspired me.

This relates to John Maxwell's Law of Contribution, which states that the ultimate goal is to grow to help others.

Chapter 1:
STEP 1: Discovering Your Passion and Purpose

The Seven Simple Steps to Joining and Thriving in Humanitarian Work

The Comprehensive Guide

Are you eager to embark on a career in the humanitarian sector but need help figuring out where to start? Fear not!

With over twenty years of experience working in thirteen countries for International non-governmental organizations, I am here to guide you through seven simple steps that will bring you or people you refer to this guidebook, closer than ever to achieving your dream job.

Welcome to my world as we begin this journey together.

STEP 1: Discovering Your Passion and Purpose

In this first step, I welcome you to unlock your potential and identify your passion for humanitarian work.

You can start by learning from my personal story and real-life experiences to ignite your purpose and commitment to serving others.

Unlocking your potential and identifying your passion for humanitarian work starts with a profound reflection on your values, interests, and aspirations aligning with humanitarian organizations' missions and values. You can learn from referrals who have gone before you. You can also learn from real-life experiences that ignite your purpose and commitment to serving others. Or you can learn from books like this guidebook.

The bottom of this enormous hill is not a walk in the park. I must have sent over fifty applications before I landed my first job with a reputable agency in Myanmar, initially on a three-month contract. My journey exemplified the importance of perseverance and determination in pursuing career aspirations despite numerous rejections and setbacks.

There are various entry points for those aspiring to contribute to international development and humanitarian efforts. Consider the following pathways to kickstart your journey.

1. **Internships:** Internships provide valuable professional learning experiences that allow you to explore different career paths, develop new skills, and gain practical experience. Whether paid or unpaid, internships offer opportunities for career development and exposure to humanitarian work.

For example, I worked as an unpaid intern as an Administrative/Finance Assistant in a refugee camp during my undergraduate degree. At the refugee camp, my role was mainly to process payments to suppliers of goods and also process travel claims for Sudanese refugees who were traveling to the Kenyan capital for interviews to allow them to resettle in countries like the United States, Sweden, and Australia. Later on, I worked as a paid intern with Womankind Worldwide in London, during my graduate studies. Gaining experience through internships provides invaluable hands-on skills, industry insights, and professional connections that significantly enhance your prospects for securing future jobs.

2. **Volunteer Opportunities:** Volunteering allows you to contribute to different programs or projects through volunteerism worldwide. You can start as a youth volunteer, national volunteer, or international volunteer.

One can also start as part of the African Union Youth Volunteer Corps and gain meaningful experience, later transitioning to other international organizations. Volunteering provides job seekers with diverse opportunities for personal growth and making a difference in the communities they serve.

3. **Deployment or Secondment:** You can serve in organizations like the Norwegian Refugee Council, Danish Refugee Council, or CANADEM- a Canadian non-profit agency that aims to advance international peace and security by rapidly mobilizing personnel and resources in

response to global crises. These organizations offer deployment or secondment opportunities for individuals to support humanitarian efforts on the ground and sometimes second people to the United Nations. They target job seekers who can provide hands-on experience in emergency response and development projects.

4. **Temporary or Renewable Contracts:** Individuals seeking to work in specific areas of expertise are offered entry through a competitive interview process. These appointments provide opportunities to contribute to ongoing projects and initiatives within the organization.

5. **Junior Professional Officer (JPO) Program:** The JPO Program offers recent graduates or young professionals the chance to work on development projects or technical assistance programs within International non-governmental organizations.

Sponsored by participating countries, JPOs receive mentorship and guidance to develop their skills and contribute to development efforts. While most are for nationals of the donor country, while working in Ethiopia, I met a Malawian sponsored by the Netherlands.

I also worked with Japanese, Norwegian, and Swedish JPOs sponsored by their countries. By the end of their third year as JPOs, most were converted to ongoing appointments.

6. **Young Professional Program (YPP):** The YPP is a recruitment initiative by international non-governmental organizations like the World Bank. It targets job seekers for entry-level positions and may include openings for recent graduates or early-career professionals. The selection process is very competitive, so applicants must position themselves as the most suitable candidate at the preparatory stage, during, and after the competency-based interviews. Successful candidates receive training, mentorship, and opportunities for career advancement within the organization.

While not exhaustive, by exploring these top six entry points and pathways, you can embark on a rewarding career journey with humanitarian organizations, contributing to global peace, development, and humanitarian assistance efforts.

Chapter 2:
STEP 2: Building a Strong Foundation

STEP 2: Building a Strong Foundation

In this step, you lay the groundwork for your journey by acquiring relevant skills, knowledge, and qualifications. You can do this by navigating the recruitment process and understanding the requirements for entry-level positions within the humanitarian world.

Laying the Groundwork: Preparing for a Career and Humanitarian Work

2.1 Crafting a Compelling Curriculum Vitae (CV) or Resume

As you embark on your journey to secure a position in humanitarian work or with related organizations, the first crucial step is to prepare a comprehensive and professional CV or resume. Your CV serves as the foundation of your application and should showcase your qualifications, experiences, and suitability for the role.

Start by crafting a concise *Summary Statement* highlighting your career objectives and critical qualifications. This section should provide a snapshot of your unique value proposition statement and demonstrate how your skills and experience align with the position requirements you are applying for.

Next, you must list your educational background chronologically, including details of the degrees, courses, and institutions you have attended. Include any relevant certifications or specialized training that may apply to the advertised role.

Carefully capture your work experience section, focusing on roles directly relevant to the position you seek. Provide job titles, dates of employment, and a summarized description of your key responsibilities and achievements.

This section should showcase your operational experience and demonstrate how you have developed the necessary skills and competencies desirable to excel in the advertised position. It is essential to highlight your language proficiency, technical skills, and other relevant competencies that may be valuable in the required context.

Additionally, some applications require contact information for references who can attest to your abilities and character, which can further strengthen your application.

By meticulously preparing your CV, you can ensure that your application stands out among the pool of candidates, showcasing your qualifications and suitability for any advertised position.

To tailor your resume to a specific job, carefully review the job description and highlight the essential skills, qualifications, and responsibilities sought by the employer. Identify the keywords used in the job description and strategically incorporate them into your resume as applicable, particularly in the summary, skills, and work experience sections, to help your resume pass through applicant tracking systems (ATS) and demonstrate your strong fit for the role.

Reorder your resume sections to prioritize relevant experiences and qualifications, placing the most aligned work experience at the top. Tailor the bullet points in your work experience to emphasize achievements and responsibilities directly applicable to the job requirements and quantify your accomplishments whenever possible.

Reviewing and constantly removing irrelevant information is essential to keep your resume concise and focused on the employer's needs. Finally, format your resume in a clean, easy-to-scan layout to make it visually appealing and highlight your qualifications. By following these steps, you can thoroughly customize your resume for each job application, demonstrating your perfect suitability for the role and increasing your chances of securing an interview.

Most organizations now have online forms that are easy to complete according to the required format using the information already prepared in the CV.

2.2 Navigating the Recruitment Process

Once you have crafted a compelling CV, the next step is to navigate the recruitment process for the humanitarian organization of interest. This process typically involves several stages designed to assess your qualifications, skills, and perfect fit for the role.

2.2.1 Understanding the Job Requirements

Carefully review the job description and requirements for the position you are applying for. Ensure that you fully understand the responsibilities, qualifications, and competencies the international non-governmental organization seeks in a successful candidate. This will allow you to tailor your application and highlight the specific ways in which your experiences and skills align with the role.

2.2.2 Addressing the Application Questions

During the application process, you may encounter questions that ask you to describe your achievements, relevant skills, and competencies, and how the role fits into your career aspirations. Prepare thoughtful, well-structured responses demonstrating your qualifications and enthusiasm for the position. Highlight specific examples from your work experience that showcase your ability to excel in the role.

2.2.3 Showcasing Your Alignment with the Role

Emphasize how your achievements, experience, and career goals align with the desired role. Demonstrate your understanding of the organization's mission and values and explain how your unique skills and experience can contribute to the team's success and the organization's overall objectives. A well-prepared approach will increase your chances of standing out.

Cover Letter Template for Humanitarian Role

Your name and address

Tailored simplified Cover Letter Template for Humanitarian Role

Date

To: Contact and Organization's Address

Dear Sir/Madam

Introduction: Express enthusiasm for the role and the organization. Briefly mention your experience and how it aligns with the organization's mission.

Highlight Relevant Experience and Skills: Mention key skills and accomplishments.

Align with Organization's Mission: Explain why you are passionate about the organization's work. Reference a program or initiative that resonates with you and how your experience relates to their mission.

Express Enthusiasm and Contribution: Convey excitement about the opportunity. Highlight how your skills and experiences can support the organization's goals.

Closing: Thank the hiring manager for their consideration in advance. Indicate your interest in discussing the role further and express your eagerness to contribute to the team.

Warmest regards,
Your name, email, and phone number

Chapter 3:
STEP 3: Navigating
the Application Process

STEP 3: Navigating the Application Process

In the previous step, you master crafting compelling resumes, cover letters, and personal statements showcasing your unique strengths and qualifications. Learn how to tailor your application to specific job vacancies and highlight your relevant experiences, skills, and achievements. Gain insider tips and strategies for standing out in a competitive job market.

There are many online applications formats, and you can utilize the following links to access a wide range of job opportunities and complete your profile.

3.1. ReliefWeb (www.reliefweb.int) Serves as an entry point for humanitarian and development jobs. They offer search options based on job type, career category, theme, experience, country, and organization type. My first three jobs with international non-governmental organizations – International Medical Corps, International Rescue Committee and Mercy Corps, and my first UN jobs with UNOCHA in Myanmar and UN Women in Ethiopia, followed my response to ads found on www.reliefweb.int.

3.2. Devnetjobs (www.devnetjobs.org) covers various job opportunities within the UN, aid organizations, NGOs, and consultancy firms in the international development community, providing a comprehensive platform for job seekers.

3.3. Inspira (www.inspira.un.org) is the official recruitment portal for the United Nations Secretariat, particularly for roles within the Secretariat and Peacekeeping missions. It offers access to job vacancies, internships, and temporary positions across different duty stations and organizations within the UN system.

3.4. UN Jobs (www.unjobs.org) is a dedicated platform for searching and applying for vacancies within the United Nations system. This site lists positions across different agencies, departments, and specialized programs.

3.5. The UN Careers (https://careers.un.org/) portal is the official recruitment website for the United Nations Secretariat. It offers a comprehensive database of job vacancies, internships, and consultancy opportunities across various functional areas and geographic locations.

I will also include three other routes which provide the necessary experience to help you join the UN.

3.6. African Union (AU) Careers (www.au.int) is an official website that offers information on career opportunities within the AU Commission and affiliated bodies. These include positions in various sectors, such as peace, security, health, education, and agriculture.

3.7. Danish Refugee Council (DRC) Standby Partnership (www.drc.standbypartnership.org) offers job seekers three specialized deployment rosters to address diverse humanitarian needs. The Humanitarian Response Roster provides professionals with opportunities for deployment to international organizations or UN operations, focusing on technical areas such as protection, logistics, humanitarian affairs, WASH, information technology, cluster coordination, and food security, typically for three to six months.

3.8. Norwegian Refugee Council (NORCAP) Roster (https://www.nrc.no)

NORCAP runs a roster for expertise in the humanitarian, peace, and development sectors, including WASH, Livelihoods, and Shelter.

3.9. CANADEM (www.canadem.ca) is relevant for professionals seeking deployment opportunities to support international peace and humanitarian operations. It also provides a platform for individuals seeking to contribute to humanitarian assistance and peace-building initiatives.

By utilizing these valuable links, job seekers can access diverse job opportunities with International Non-profit and affiliated organizations, helping them find positions that align with their skills, experience, and career aspirations.

Chapter 4:
STEP 4: Preparing
for Interviews

STEP 4: Preparing for Interviews

In this step, you will master the STARL technique (Situation, Task, Action, Result, Learning) to ace your interviews with confidence and poise. You will prepare for competency-based interviews by showcasing your problem-solving skills, leadership abilities, and cultural awareness.

Discover how to effectively communicate your experiences and demonstrate your suitability for the advertised roles.

Navigating Competency-Based Interviews (CBIs), crucial for International organizations roles, requires grasping their structure and purpose. CBIs assess problem-solving abilities through open-ended questions grounded in the belief that past experiences can predict future performance.

However, not all experiences may directly translate; hence, the focus is on specific competencies. The 'four-fold' approach to CBIs involves evaluating past roles' alignment with future responsibilities, contributions, challenges faced, achieved results, and lessons learned.

These interviews typically cover a competency framework, including critical values, core values, managerial skills, and cross-functional abilities. Preparation entails understanding the job description, practicing responses using the STARL technique (Situation, Task, Action, Result, Learning), testing technical equipment, dressing professionally, and maintaining confidence and engagement during the interview.

Essential strategies include referencing competencies from the Terms of Reference, maintaining engagement through pitch and tone (for phone interviews), and creating a positive first impression (for face-to-face interviews).

I gained valuable insight from an online resource: Michel Emery's YouTube video on UN recruitment, recorded in 2013 when he was the Director for Human Resources at the United Nations Population Fund (UNFPA). The video can be found at the YouTube link, and is entitled Competency Based Interviewing on YouTube.

As a job seeker, understanding the key competencies employers seek is essential for effectively preparing for interviews and highlighting your suitability for the role. The competency framework typically covers four main categories:

4.1. Key Values: Employers often seek candidates who demonstrate integrity, professionalism, and respect for diversity. These values are fundamental to fostering a positive work environment and promoting ethical behavior within the organization.

4.2. Core Values: Accountability, teamwork, communication, continuous learning, client and results orientation, and organizational awareness are core competencies employers seek. These values reflect an individual's ability to work collaboratively, communicate effectively, adapt to changing circumstances, and deliver results aligned with the organization's goals.

4.3. Managerial Skills: For leadership roles or positions requiring managerial responsibilities, employers look for competencies such as empowering and building trust among team members, effective managerial performance, sound judgment, decision-making abilities, strategic planning, vision leadership, and efficient resource management. These skills are essential for the organization's success and lead teams toward achieving their objectives.

4.4. Cross-Functional Abilities: Most employers value candidates who possess cross-functional competencies. These include analytical thinking, innovation and creativity, technological awareness, negotiation and conflict resolution skills, stakeholder management, policy research and development capabilities, and change capability and adaptability. These competencies enable individuals to navigate complex challenges, drive innovation, and effectively engage with stakeholders to achieve organizational objectives.

When seeking employment, it is vital to recognize that competency and proficiency requirements can differ based on the job level and specific role. Job descriptions are invaluable resources, detailing each position's expected competencies and proficiencies. Aligning your skills and experience with these critical competencies enhances your candidacy and boosts your chances of success in the job search process. As a key tip, prepare three to four interchangeable scenarios using the STARL technique to respond to multiple competencies. One example suitable for Accountability can also be ideal for Teamwork and Communication. For higher-level roles, avoid transactional examples but be more strategic, highlighting an innovative solution you created to solve a problem faced by several stakeholders. Highlight the situation. What was the task, the action you took, the results, and any lesson learned?

Chapter 5:
STEP 5: Thriving in
the Field

STEP 5: Thriving in the Field

Next, you must learn to navigate the complexities of working in diverse cultural, political, and humanitarian environments. I had to learn and relearn strategies for adapting to new cultures, building relationships with colleagues and stakeholders, and overcoming challenges with resilience and determination. Gain practical tips for managing stress, maintaining work-life balance, and staying motivated in demanding situations.

Let me share my journey of surviving and thriving as a humanitarian worker, as it might resonate with your aspirations. Working in humanitarian work demands unique skills and strategies to navigate its dynamic and challenging environment. Firstly, resilience and adaptability are paramount, given the complex challenges and frequent changes in assignments or locations.

I was working in Darfur during President Bashir's expulsion of fourteen American and British NGOs, including Mercy Corps. This disruption of aid efforts left vulnerable communities in dire need. As the Head of Finance for Mercy Corps Darfur, I led by swiftly implementing our business continuity plan to ensure operational continuity while facing restricted access and heightened insecurity.

The subsequent government demand for additional salaries, totaling hundreds of thousands of dollars, posed a formidable challenge. Despite facing intimidation and bureaucratic hurdles, we navigated negotiations with resilience and determination, eventually securing the necessary funds to pay staff salaries.

This experience taught me the importance of maintaining composure in crisis situations, escalating challenges for support, and leveraging collaborative efforts to overcome obstacles.

Surviving and thriving as a humanitarian worker requires resilience, adaptability, and a deep commitment to continuous learning. My journey has been filled with challenges, from navigating cultural differences in conflict zones to overcoming setbacks that tested my determination. But through perseverance, I have discovered that each obstacle has strengthened my resolve and deepened my passion for making a difference. I invite you to share my story, learn from the struggles and triumphs I experienced, and find inspiration in your path. Here are some of the seven key tips which will help you thrive in the feel and create an impact fueled by our collective determination.

Firstly, developing strong communication skills, both verbal and written, is crucial for collaborating effectively with colleagues from diverse backgrounds. Additionally, fostering cultural sensitivity and empathy enables successful interactions with individuals from distinct cultures and communities, aligning with international non-governmental organizations' commitment to diversity and inclusion.

Next is continuous self-improvement which has been critical to my success in humanitarian work. Investing in professional development opportunities, such as training programs and workshops, has helped me enhance my skills and knowledge base. This year alone I was certified as a John Maxwell Leadership Coach and in Artificial Intelligence by AI Innovision.

I gained invaluable skills that benefit me and trickle down to the teams I supervise indirectly. It pays to invest in personal development which often comes at your own cost but pays off. Actively seeking feedback from supervisors and peers has also facilitated my personal growth and identified areas for improvement.

Thirdly is prioritizing work-life balance and self-care, which has been essential for maintaining my well-being and sustaining productivity in the demanding humanitarian environment. I value my seven days of Rest and Recuperation (R&R), which is available to allow humanitarian workers to recharge physically and mentally, especially in challenging environments.

Additionally, language proficiency is highly valued in international organizations, with proficiency in English being typically required for most positions. However, proficiency in additional languages relevant to specific regions or countries of operation can significantly enhance competitiveness and effectiveness in your role. English, French, Spanish, Arabic, Russian and Chinese are the common languages, for most International Organizations, which serves as the forth tip.

Recognizing the need to enhance my language skills was pivotal in my professional journey. As I aspired for a position in Francophone countries, I understood that proficiency in French was not just a requirement but a key asset for effective regional communication and collaboration.

Despite the geographical barriers that separated me from a traditional classroom setting, I embraced the wealth of online resources available. I sought guidance from an esteemed tutor, Mr Tony Ancient, whose contact information I obtained online from preplay (https://preply.com). Tony's tutorials were complemented by an online resource, an annual subscription to Learn French with Alexa (learnfrenchwithalexa.com).

Through tailored lessons and my unwavering dedication, I achieved proficiency at the B2 level within a relatively short timeframe. I was interviewed in French for my post in Cameroon, and I nailed it. I later understood my competitor was French, but combining my experience, competency, and the desired level of French, earned me an upper edge and a job offer to serve in a more senior role.

This experience underscored the importance of learning additional skills and languages for career growth. In today's globalized world, where borders are increasingly blurred, proficiency in multiple languages is not merely advantageous but essential.

Multilingualism enhances job prospects and fosters cross-cultural understanding and collaboration. It will open your doors to new opportunities, expand professional networks, and equip you with the confidence and competence to navigate diverse environments.

Of great importance is building and nurturing professional networks has been critical for thriving as a relief worker, which is my sixth but possibly the most important tip. Engaging with colleagues, participating in internal working groups or committees, and attending relevant conferences or events have fostered connections and facilitated knowledge sharing.

This reflects John Maxwell's Law of Environment, which emphasizes the importance of surrounding yourself with supportive people and growth opportunities. Additionally, leveraging external networks, such as partnerships with other organizations and academic institutions, has expanded my opportunities for collaboration and learning.

Surviving and thriving as a humanitarian worker requires a combination of resilience, adaptability, continuous learning, effective communication, language proficiency, and strategic networking. By focusing on personal and professional development, maintaining a healthy work-life balance, and embracing diverse career paths, you can successfully navigate the challenges and opportunities inherent in the sector.

Lastly, it is important to believe in yourself and your dreams and not limit yourself to one job or career path. There are options to explore multiple paths, including

Headquarter and field experiences. You may find yourself in Hungary or attend a training in Rome, Geneva or New York, or find yourself in Kabul, Nyala or Addis Ababa like I did. All these paths can open doors wide for invaluable growth and opportunities within relief work and beyond. Welcome to my world.

Chapter 6:
STEP 6: Unlock a World of Opportunities, Impact and Rewards

STEP 6: Unlock a World of Opportunities, Impact and Rewards

To unlock the limitless opportunities in the humanitarian sector, it is essential to take deliberate steps toward personal and professional growth. I offer additional tips to guide you on this journey. First, commit to lifelong learning and professional development to thrive in your career with international non-governmental organizations. By exploring opportunities for continuing or furthering your education, training, and certification, you will expand your skills and expertise, keeping yourself adaptable in an ever-changing field. I learnt to continuously cultivate a growth mindset and embraced challenges as opportunities, which further fueled my personal and professional growth.

Additionally, harness your passion, skills, and experiences to make a positive impact within the humanitarian workforce and beyond. I have had to engage in meaningful projects, initiatives, and collaborations that not only align with my organization's mission but also contribute to sustainable development and peace-building efforts globally. By mirroring these shared lessons from my experience, you too will inspire others to join this impactful journey and become changemakers themselves, fostering a broader movement for lasting change.

Working with international non-governmental organizations is a rewarding experience that offers competitive salaries and opportunities for professional growth. As you consider potential roles within the organization, it is important to explore how these benefits align with your needs and aspirations, the opportunity it brings, the impact you can create, and the benefits you will get as a reward.

6.1. Global Impact: As a Humanitarian worker, you too can make a positive impact on key global issues such as peacekeeping, humanitarian aid, sustainable development, human rights, and climate change. This work enables individuals to help address some of the world's most critical challenges.

6.2. Diverse and Inclusive Work Environment: Humanitarian work promotes diversity, equality, and inclusion, offering a respectful environment where individuals from all backgrounds collaborate. Employees benefit from working with colleagues of various nationalities and disciplines, enhancing cross-cultural understanding and cooperation. You too can benefit from serving in several countries overseas or even more and always work with other professionals from many different nationalities, thereby broadening my view of the world.

6.3. Professional Development Opportunities: The sector offers numerous opportunities for professional growth and development, including training programs, workshops, seminars, and learning resources. As an employee, you will have access to career advancement opportunities, mentorship programs, and skill-building initiatives that enables you to enhance their expertise and progress in their careers.

6.4. Competitive Compensation and Benefits: Humanitarian staff receive competitive salaries and comprehensive benefits packages that may include health insurance, retirement plans, paid leave, and other allowances. These benefits help ensure employees' and their families' well-being and financial security.

6.5. International Experience: Working for international non-governmental organizations provides the opportunity to gain valuable international experience and exposure to diverse cultures, languages, and environments. I have worked in thirteen duty stations worldwide, from Yemen to Afghanistan, from Budapest in Hungary to Cameroon, from Yemen to Iraq, and in many more field offices. You too can enrich your professional and personal experiences beyond borders.

6.6. Networking and Collaboration: The humanitarian sector offers extensive networking opportunities for staff to engage with colleagues, experts, and stakeholders from governments, civil society, academia, and the private sector. I have had the invaluable opportunity to immerse myself in extensive networking avenues that facilitated connections with a wide range of stakeholders globally.

One of the most pivotal experiences during my tenure in Ethiopia was when I took on the role of Chairperson for the Operations Management Committee. This position significantly expanded my professional network and deepened my understanding of the importance of leveraging these connections for growth. Jointly with my core chairs, we coordinated the intricate logistics of the African Union Summit, managing everything from the accreditation process for the Secretary General's delegation to overseeing VIP passes with the Ministry of Foreign Affairs.

Beyond this, I had the honor of orchestrating logistics for a gathering of African Women Ministers from fifty-two countries, African queens, civil society organizations, and academia. This role also required me to coordinate the evacuations of staff members from neighboring countries, utilizing Ethiopia as a strategic hub for regional connectivity.

Through these diverse and challenging tasks, I continued to learn the immense value of collaboration and networking. Working with a wide array of partners as is typical in international Organizations, will allow you to harness collective expertise and resources, which is crucial in successfully achieving any shared objectives, no matter where you work.

In today's interconnected world, building and leveraging a strong professional network is not just an advantage—it's essential for achieving your career goals. Networking opens doors to new opportunities, provides access to valuable resources, and enables you to collaborate with others who can help you reach your objectives. Whether you are just starting in your career or looking to advance, make a conscious effort to build relationships with colleagues, mentors, and industry professionals. Attend conferences, join professional groups, and actively engage in your community. By investing in your network, you will not only expand your reach but also enhance your ability to make a meaningful impact in your chosen field.

6.7. A Sense of Purpose and Fulfillment: As you embark on your job search journey, consider the profound fulfillment awaiting you within an organization committed to advancing peace, human rights, social justice, and sustainable development.

Contributing to meaningful causes and serving as a powerful motivator for employees gives one an unparalleled sense of purpose. Drawing from my own experiences, I have had the privilege of providing logistical support to displaced persons, ranging from the stateless Rohingya in Myanmar to refugees and internally displaced persons (IDPs) in Sudan and Cameroon.

Witnessing the impact of our efforts firsthand and knowing that each action contributes to alleviating suffering and fostering positive change is incredibly rewarding. As you seek opportunities, prioritize organizations whose values align with your own, and remember the profound sense of fulfillment that comes from making a difference in the lives of others.

6.8. Work-Life Balance:

As you explore various opportunities and consider your next career move, it is crucial to prioritize your well-being and maintain a healthy work-life balance. Like many reputable organizations, international non-governmental organizations recognize the significance of this balance and have implemented policies and programs to support employees in managing their professional and personal responsibilities. These initiatives include flexible work arrangements, parental leave, and other supportive measures to promote your well-being and satisfaction.

In addition, for those based in hardship locations, international non-governmental organizations acknowledge the importance of regular breaks to ensure employees have time to reconnect with their families and recharge. Therefore, depending on the hardship faced in your duty station, you should have the opportunity to take time off to see your loved ones every four to twelve weeks.

When you join Humanitarian work, always remember that maintaining a healthy work-life balance helps prevent unnecessary stress and contributes to your overall health and happiness. As you explore career opportunities, prioritize organizations that value your well-being and offer the necessary support to help you personally and professionally thrive.

Overall, working for the humanitarian sector will provide you with a unique opportunity to make a difference on a global scale, grow professionally, and be part of a diverse and inclusive community committed to creating a better world for all.

As you explore opportunities, I will also help you understand the attractive benefits and numeration available to employees. Most available roles come with a range of benefits designed to support your well-being and enhance your overall experience. Here is an overview of some of the key benefits you can expect while noting that the available range differs from one organization to another:

1. **Medical Insurance:** Comprehensive medical coverage for you and your eligible dependents, ensuring access to quality healthcare services.

2. **Education:** Assistance for qualified dependents and children's educational expenses, including tuition fees and related costs, beyond borders. You may be in Haiti but send your child to study in Geneva with a huge part of the tuition covered beyond borders.

3. **Paid Travel:** Support for travel expenses related to the travel of eligible staff and their eligible dependents, facilitating access to various locations and opportunities.

4. **Paid Trips Home:** From my NGO experience, I earned eligibility for periodic travel allowances, which allowed me to reconnect with family and loved ones regularly.

5. **Flights for Official Travel:** Coverage of flights for official travel related to your role within international non-governmental organizations, is provided, thereby ensuring seamless movement for work purposes.

6. **Hazardous Allowance:** This is additional compensation for some employees working in

hazardous or challenging environments, recognizing the risks associated with certain assignments. Other organizations will offer you an additional allowance as compensation for working away from their families.

7. **Mobility Allowance:** when transitioning to new locations, you may be eligible for some financial assistance to support your movement-related expenses.

8. **Shipment:** Humanitarian agencies offer assistance with relocating to a new duty station, including shipment of personal belongings and related expenses.

9. **Education Opportunities:** Access is provided towards professional development and paid educational opportunities beyond borders to enhance your skills and knowledge.

10. **Special Leave with or without Pay:** You may be eligible for special leave with full pay for specific circumstances, ensuring support during critical times, for example, to pursue further studies, including seeking foreign language skills enhancement abroad, in some organizations.

11. **Rest and Recuperation (R&R):** Periodic breaks and allowances are available to promote Rest and recuperation for some employees deployed in challenging environments. In the NGO, I received

a break every nine weeks. Other Humanitarian agencies offer breaks every four, six, eight or twelve weeks, depending on the level of hardship in the location where you serve.

12. **Vacation and Holidays:** You will receive generous annual leave entitlements depending on your contract of service to promote work-life balance and well-being. On average, two to two and a half days are given monthly. The holidays are prioritized while respecting diversity by including a few days for different religions, which varies from country to country.

13. **Transportation Allowance:** Most international organizations offer transportation expenses, facilitating commuting to and from work, especially for international staff. The same may be extended to national staff through carpool shuttles on a subsidized cost-recovery basis.

14. **Accommodation:** Access to accommodation options or allowances to support housing needs at a subsidized rate will be available if you are deployed to a hardship location with house shortages.

15. **Flexible Working Arrangements:** Opportunities for flexible work arrangements is an option you will have in most cases, to accommodate personal needs and optimize productivity.

16. **Dependent Benefit:** When evaluating potential employment opportunities, it is essential for job seekers to consider the benefits available for their dependents, including children and the official spouse. These benefits can provide comprehensive support for eligible family members, ensuring their well-being while they focus on their careers.

These benefits, along with competitive salaries and opportunities for professional growth, make working with international non-governmental organizations a rewarding experience.

Chapter 7:
STEP 7: Having an
Exit Strategy

STEP 7: Having an Exit Strategy

In this final step, you must learn how to transition into retirement through early retirement planning, borrowing from what I learnt from colleagues and affiliates over the years. Organizations like international non-governmental organizations recognize the importance of supporting staff throughout their entire career lifecycle, including during retirement.

By providing resources, information, and support, they ensure that staff members can enjoy a fulfilling and successful retirement experience, depending on what is available.

Retirement is a significant milestone in any career journey, and for most humanitarian staff, it is a transition that is supported comprehensively to ensure a fulfilling and successful retirement experience.

Here are some helpful beginner's tips for retirement planning and support based on what is available for international non-governmental organizations. Keep in mind that the benefits offered differ from organization to organization:

7.1. Retirement Options: International non-governmental organizations employees have several retirement options, including early or regular retirement. Eligibility criteria and benefits associated with each option may vary based on age, years of service, and pension plan participation. Retirement is generally allowable from fifty-five to sixty-five years of age.

7.2. Pension Benefits: On average, employees contribute five to eight per cent of their pensionable remuneration to pension funds, which the employer matches double. These contributions are crucial in funding the pension fund and ensuring the sustainability of retirement benefits.

Upon retirement, the benefits offer retirement, disability, and survivor benefits based on the years of service, salary, and contribution rates.

7.3. Health Insurance Coverage: In some organizations, retired staff may continue participating in health insurance plans, ensuring access to quality healthcare post-retirement.

7.4. Financial Planning and Counseling: International non-governmental organizations provide retirement planning services and financial counseling to help staff members make informed decisions about retirement finances, investments, and estate planning.

7.5. Post-Retirement Employment Opportunities: Retirees may pursue post-retirement employment opportunities for a limited amount of time, with some international organizations offering options for occasional consultancy services for retired staff. This could be for two to six months annually based on your availability.

7.6. Social and Community Support: International non-governmental organizations encourage retirees to stay connected through social activities, clubs, and networks organized through employee welfare associations, fostering community, and belonging.

7.7. Counseling and Mental Health Support: Retirement can bring emotional challenges, and organizations may provide counseling services and mental health support to retirees and their families to address concerns and navigate lifestyle adjustments.

7.8. Access to Resources and Information: Retirees have access to resources and information through relevant communication channels, which provide updates on retirement benefits, opportunities, and services.

By providing the necessary support, even as one transitions into retirement, it is possible to maintain well-being and stay connected with the humanitarian community throughout one's retirement years. However, as a useful tip it is crucial to remember that the security of your future is NOT solely dependent on organizational support—your personal preparedness plays an equally vital role.

Whatever you do, even during your active working life, never forget to save for rainy days. From my many years, I know beyond any reasonable doubt that emergencies have a way of creeping up when you least expect them, often at the most inconvenient times. By setting aside funds regularly, you can ensure that you are financially prepared to handle unforeseen circumstances without undue stress.

In a mastermind I once took in Harve Eker's Academy, we explored the Seven Jars, which taught me the importance of balancing and nurturing essential areas of life—personal growth, relationships, work, health, finances, fun, and spirituality—to achieve lasting fulfillment and success.

Start saving a portion of your income, no matter how small, to build a safety net for those unpredictable moments. Your future self will thank you for the foresight and discipline to secure your financial well-being. The good news is that so many of us have gone before you, like my mentors and me, and are willing to hold your hand, mentor, and coach you to make it easier when you reach out.

Conclusion:
You are Called to
Serve Across Borders

In conclusion, despite the challenges posed by reduced funding and competing needs, humanitarian work is a shining example and one of the greatest opportunities for those passionate about making a tangible difference in the world.

Now, more than ever, the need for dedicated individuals to fill the gaps in humanitarian development and peace-building efforts is critical. By joining Humanitarian work, you become part of a global community committed to addressing humanity's most pressing challenges, serve in Ukraine, Haiti, Sudan or Lebanon, offering the much-needed support from conflicts to climate change and pandemics and in peace building efforts.

Working with charities offers many benefits that make it an attractive employer compared to other organizations. From unparalleled opportunities for professional growth and development to access to diverse networks and resources, the available options and networks provide a platform for you to contribute your skills and expertise toward meaningful impact on a global scale.

Moreover, the international organization's commitment to promoting inclusivity, diversity, and gender equality ensures that every voice is heard and valued, fostering a culture of collaboration and innovation, where condusive enabling environments exist.

By choosing to serve in humanitarian work, you embark on a fulfilling career and become part of a larger mission to create a more just, peaceful, and sustainable world for future generations.

If you are driven by a desire to make a difference and are ready to embrace the challenges and opportunities of humanitarian work, I welcome you to consider serving international non-governmental organizations or international aid agencies.

You will become a part of the more significant impact needed to support people caught in emergencies such as natural disasters, wars, and other crises. You will be able to contribute toward essential services and aid, including medical care, food and water supply, shelter, sanitation, and education, all aimed at alleviating human suffering and maintaining human dignity as you partner with like-minded partners in building a better future for all.

As taught by John Maxwell's Law of Contribution, the ultimate goal should be to grow to help others.

SILPER PESA

Workbook

Welcome to the Workbook for Crossing Borders: A Job Seeker's Guide to Humanitarian Work – Your Essential Companion.

This workbook is more than just a guide—it is your bridge, toolkit, and mentor on your journey toward a fulfilling career in humanitarian work. Designed to transform your ambitions into reality, it equips you with the insights, exercises, and tools needed to become a true change maker. Here's how you can maximize its potential:

SILPER PESA

Workbook for Crossing Borders

A Job Seeker's Guide to Humanitarian Work – Your Essential Companion.

Why This Workbook Will Transform Your Journey:

Engage Actively: Each section is crafted to help you understand yourself and your purpose. Dive deeply into every Step and exercise to broaden your skills and passion.

Call to Action: Share your experiences as you progress. Inspire others with your journey!

Utilize Reflection Prompts: Use the prompts to gain clarity about your motivations and goals. This self-reflection is key to articulating your aspirations.

Pro Tip: Keep a separate journal to track your growth. It's a valuable resource to revisit as your journey unfolds.

Connect and Network: The workbook encourages building relationships in the humanitarian sector. Engage with mentors, peers, and professionals to enrich your journey.

Call to Action: Aim for at least three informational interviews by the end. Learn from others who've walked this path.

Set Clear, Achievable Goals: Use this workbook as a blueprint to set realistic, actionable goals that keep you focused and motivated.

Pro Tip: Break goals into steps. If you want field experience, list steps like volunteering or networking to achieve it.

Explore Resources Provided: Each Step includes resources to expand your understanding of humanitarian work. Treat them as your treasure map to opportunities.

Call to Action: Dedicate time weekly to explore these resources and deepen your knowledge.

Revisit and Reflect: This workbook is a living document. Regularly revisit it to reflect on your progress, adjust goals, and celebrate achievements.

Pro Tip: Schedule quarterly check-ins to update your journey and recalibrate your focus.

Get Started Today!

This workbook is your catalyst for change. It's designed to help you transform your aspirations into a purposeful, impactful career. Don't just read it—immerse yourself. Take action, set goals, and connect with others. Your journey into humanitarian work starts here.

Take Action Now: Pick up your copy of Crossing Borders: A Job Seeker's Guide to Humanitarian Work and begin your journey. The world needs your passion, skills, and story—let us make it count!

Purpose

Purpose: This workbook is designed to help you apply the insights and strategies from "Crossing Borders" to your own journey in humanitarian work. Each section corresponds to the Steps in the book, providing exercises, reflection prompts, and resources for deeper exploration.

Chapter 8:
Section 1: Discovering
Your Passion and Purpose

Exercise 1: Reflect on your motivations for pursuing humanitarian work. Write down three personal experiences that have shaped this desire.

Call to Action: Connect with a mentor or someone in the field. Use the networking strategies outlined in Step 2 to schedule an informational interview.

Resource Reference: Check out the links provided in Steps one to seven of the book for organizations that can help you explore your interests further.

Objective:

By the end of this section, you will have a clearer understanding of your personal motivations and how your experiences align with a career in humanitarian work.

Exercise 1:
Reflecting on Your Motivations

Take some time to reflect on what drives you to pursue a career in humanitarian work. Write down three of your personal experiences that have shaped your desire to enter this field. Consider moments in your life where you felt a strong urge to help others, make a difference, or be part of something bigger than yourself.

Write Your Reflections Here:

1. _____

2. _____

3. _____

Reflection Prompt:

After writing your experiences, reflect on the following question: What core values or principles do these experiences reveal about you?

Write Your Reflection Here:

1. _____

2. _____

3. _____

Exercise 2:
Connecting Passion to Purpose

Now that you have identified your key motivations, let's bridge the gap between your passion and the actual work.

Identify three areas of humanitarian work that align with your passions. Use the categories provided in Step 1 of 'Crossing Borders' as a guide (e.g., disaster relief, human rights, refugee assistance, healthcare, Volunteerism, Internship etc.).

Write Your Choices Here:

1. _____

2. _____

3. _____

Exercise 3:
Call to Action: Building Connections

To gain real-world insight, use the networking strategies discussed in Step 2.

Task: Reach out to a mentor or someone currently working in humanitarian aid and schedule an informational interview.

Action Step: Write down the name of the person you plan to contact and your goal for the conversation.

Write the Name and Goals Here:

Name: _____

Goal: _____

_____

_____

Resource Reference:

In Step 1, we provided links to organizations that can help you explore your interests further. Take a moment to visit their websites and gather information on what type of roles they offer.

Task: Write down the names of two organizations that resonate with your areas of interest and what you discovered about them.

Organization 1:

Name: _____

Key Insights: _____

Organization 2:

Name: _____

Key Insights: _____

Progress Check: How confident do you feel about your understanding of your motivations for pursuing humanitarian work?

Select one:
- Very Confident

- Somewhat Confident

- Not Confident Yet

What's the most valuable takeaway from this section?

_____

_____

_____

By completing these exercises, you've taken the first step in aligning your passion and purpose with a career in humanitarian work. Keep moving forward as you explore new opportunities and connections!

Chapter 9:
Section 2: Building
a Strong Foundation

Exercise 2: Create a skills inventory by listing your current skills and identifying at least three areas for improvement relevant to humanitarian work.

Action Step: Research two organizations mentioned in Step 3 that align with your skills and values. Write down how you can contribute to their missions.

_____

_____

_____

Resource Reference: Utilize the recommended training programs and online courses listed in Step 3 to enhance your skills.

Chapter 10:
Section 3: Navigating
the Application Process

Checklist: Develop a checklist for application materials (resume, cover letter, references) based on the guidelines in Step 2.

_____

_____

_____

_____

_____

_____

Exercise 3: Draft a tailored cover letter for a specific humanitarian role you are interested in. Use the templates provided in Step 2 as a guide.

Chapter 11:
Section 4: Preparing
for Interviews

Mock Interview Questions: Review common online resources for competencies listed in Step 4. Choose four questions on key values, core values, and cross-sectional competencies and write out your answers.

1. _____

_____

2. _____

_____

3. _____

_____

4. _____

_____

Conduct a mock interview with a friend or mentor, focusing on articulating your experiences and motivations effectively.

_____

_____

_____

Register for a Live event on LinkedIn for Competency Based Interviews and Assessments.

_____

_____

_____

Chapter 12:
Section 5: Thriving in
the Field

Reflection Activity: Write about a time you faced adversity. How did you overcome it? What did you learn about yourself?

_____

_____

_____

Goal Setting: Set three professional goals for your first year in humanitarian work. Refer back to Step 5 for examples of achievable goals.

1. _____

2. _____

3. _____

Chapter 13:
Section 6: Unlocking Opportunities

Networking Exercise: Identify five people in your network who work in humanitarian roles. Reach out to them using the tips from Step 6 for informational interviews.

Resource List: Compile a list of online resources, websites, and platforms for job searching mentioned in Step 6.

1. _____

2. _____

3. _____

4. _____

5. _____

6. _____

7. _____

Chapter 14:
Section 7: Crafting
an Exit Strategy

Future Planning Worksheet: Outline your long-term career goals and potential exit strategies when transitioning out of a humanitarian role, as discussed in Step 7.

Reflection Questions:

1. What legacy do you want to leave in your humanitarian career?

_____

_____

_____

2. How can you continue contributing after leaving a role.

_____

_____

_____

Afterword

Read about John C Maxwell's 'Law of Intentionality" from the 15 Invaluable Laws of growth and write three of your reflections here.

1. _____

_____

2. _____

_____

3. _____

_____

Revisit the workbook section periodically as you progress in your career remembering that growth is a continuous journey filled with opportunities for learning and connection.

About the Author

Silper has dedicated her career to humanitarian work, impacting lives across 13 countries. With a passion for helping others unlock their potential in the sector, she became a John Maxwell Leadership certified coach and was AI certified by AI InnoVison in 2024. Silper combines her personal experience with practical advice to inspire and elevate the next generation of humanitarian workers and invite you too to "cross borders'.

www.ingramcontent.com/pod-product-compliance
Lightning Source LLC
Chambersburg PA
CBHW021537260326
41914CB00001B/47